THE FABULOUS LOST & FOUND

AND THE LITTLE DUTCH MOUSE

WRITTEN BY MARK PALLIS
ILLUSTRATED BY PETER BAYNTON

NEU WESTEND
— PRESS —

For Emily and Lucy - MP

For Hannah and Skye - PB

THE FABULOUS LOST & FOUND AND THE LITTLE DUTCH MOUSE
Copyright text © 2020 Mark Pallis and Copyright images © 2020 Peter Baynton

First Printing in the UK, 2020
ISBN 978-1-9160801-4-0
NeuWestendPress.com

THE
FABULOUS
LOST &
FOUND

AND THE LITTLE DUTCH MOUSE

WRITTEN BY MARK PALLIS
ILLUSTRATED BY PETER BAYNTON

NEU WESTEND
— PRESS —

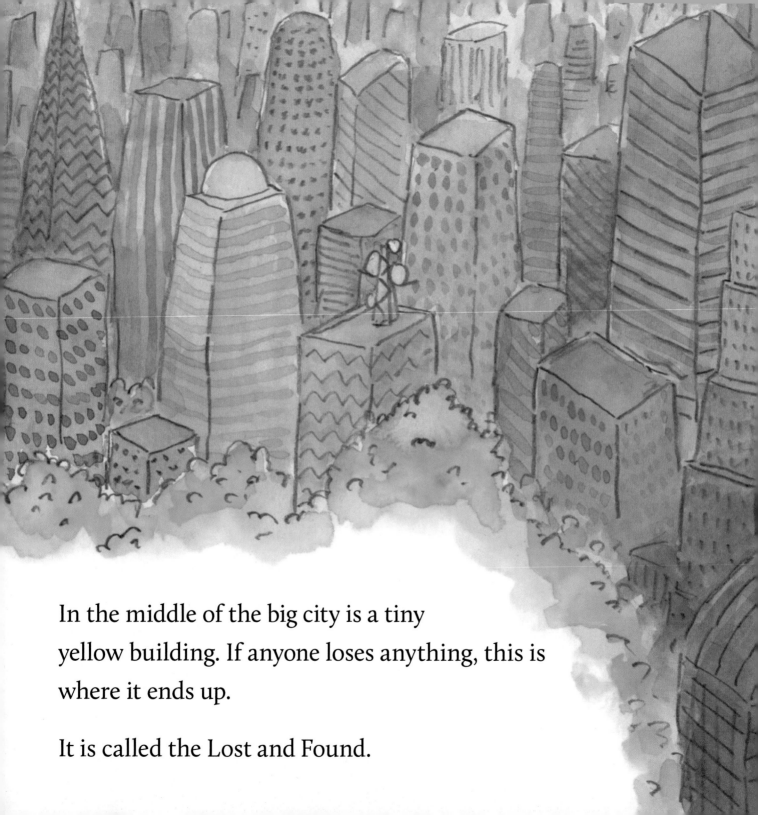

In the middle of the big city is a tiny yellow building. If anyone loses anything, this is where it ends up.

It is called the Lost and Found.

Mr and Mrs Frog keep everything safe, hoping that someday every lost watch and bag and phone and toy and shoe and cheesegrater will find its owner again.

But the shop is very small. And there are so many lost things. It is all quite a squeeze, but still, it's fabulous.

One sunny day, a little mouse walked in.

"Welcome," said Mrs Frog. "What have you lost?"

"Ik ben mijn hoed kwijt," said the mouse.

Mr and Mrs Frog could not speak Dutch. They had no idea what the little mouse was saying.

What shall we do? they wondered.

Maybe she's lost an umbrella. Everyone loses an umbrella at least twice, thought Mr Frog.

"Have you lost this?" asked Mr Frog.

"Een paraplu? Nee," replied the mouse.

Then Mrs Frog remembered something
that had been handed in a few months ago...

"Is this yours?" Mrs Frog asked, holding up a chunk of cheese.

"Kaas? Nee. Het stinkt!" said the mouse.

"Time to put that cheese in the bin dear," said Mr Frog.

"Maybe the word 'hoed' means coat," said Mr Frog.

"Now where did I put that nice
yellow one?"

"Got it!" said Mr Frog.

"Een jas? Nee. Ik ben mijn hoed kwijt," said the mouse.

She was starting to feel a bit frustrated.

"We need to keep trying," said Mrs Frog.

Geen sjaal.

Geen broek.

Geen trui.

Geen zonnebril.

Geen schoenen.

"Ik ben mijn hoed kwijt," said the mouse.

Geen twee fietsen.

Geen computer.

Geen drie boeken.

Geen vier bananen.

Geen vijf sleutels.

It was no good. A fat wet tear rolled
down the mouse's cheek.

"How about a nice cup of tea?" asked Mrs Frog kindly.

"Ik vind thee erg lekker. Bedankt," replied the mouse.
They sat together, sipping their tea and all feeling a bit sad.

Suddenly, the mouse realised she could try pointing.

She pointed at her head.
"Hoed!" she said.

"I've got it!" exclaimed Mrs Frog, leaping up.

"A wig of course!" said Mrs Frog.

"Geen pruik," said the mouse.

Niet rood.

Niet blond.

Niet bruin.

Niet veelkleurig.

Niet groen.

"What about this?"
asked Mr Frog, pulling back
a curtain.

"Hoed!" exclaimed the
mouse.

"Ah, so 'hoed' means hat.
Wonderful!" Mr and Mrs
Frog cheered.

Te hoog.

Te klein.

Te strak.

Te groot.

"One hat left," said
Mrs Frog, reaching all
the way to the back of the
cupboard.

"It couldn't be this
old thing, could it?"

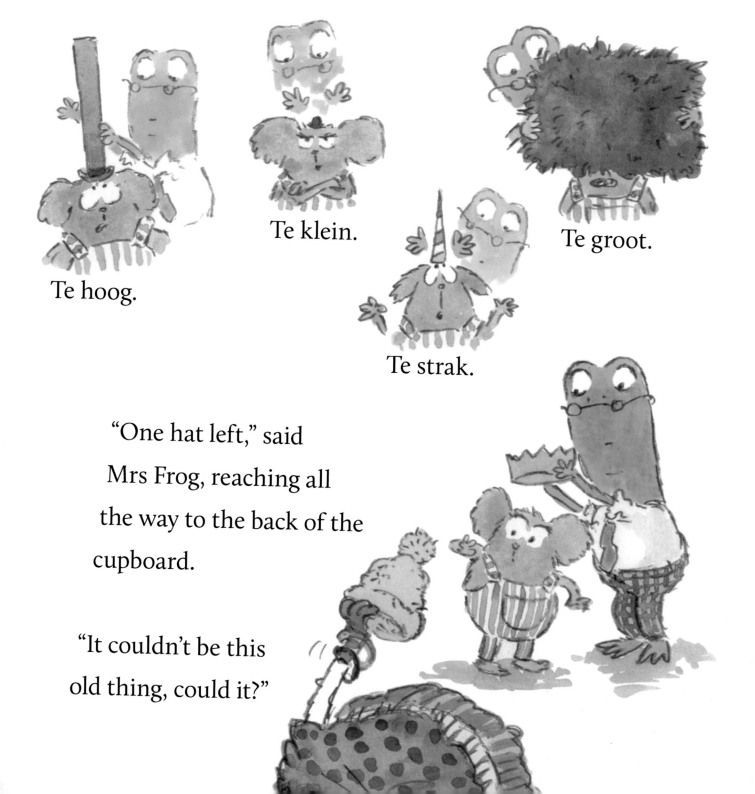

"Mijn hoed.

Ik heb mijn hoed gevonden!

Heel erg bedankt," said the mouse.

And just like that, the mouse found her hat.

"Tot ziens," she said, as she skipped away.
"Tot ziens," replied Mr and Mrs Frog.

"I wonder who will come tomorrow?" said Mr Frog.
Mrs Frog put her arm around him.

"I don't know," she replied, giving him a squeeze,
"but whoever it is, we'll do our best to help."

LEARNING TO LOVE LANGUAGES

An additional language opens a child's mind, broadens their horizons and enriches their emotional life. Research has shown that the time between a child's birth and their sixth or seventh birthday is a "golden period" when they are most receptive to new languages. This is because they have an in-built ability to distinguish the sounds they hear and make sense of them. The Story-powered Language Learning Method taps into these natural abilities.

HOW THE STORY-POWERED LANGUAGE LEARNING METHOD WORKS

We create an emotionally engaging and funny story for children and adults to enjoy together, just like any other picture book. Studies show that social interaction, like enjoying a book together, is critical in language learning.

Through the story, we introduce a relatable character who speaks only in the new language. This helps build empathy and a positive attitude towards people who speak different languages. These are both important aspects in laying the foundations for lasting language acquisition in a child's life.

As the story progresses, the child naturally works with the characters to discover the meanings of a wide range of fun new words. Strategic use of humour ensures that this subconscious learning is rewarded with laughter; the child feels good and the first seeds of a lifelong love of languages are sown.

For more information and free downloads visit www.neuwestendpress.com

ALL THE BEAUTIFUL DUTCH WORDS AND PHRASES FROM OUR STORY

ik ben mijn hoed kwijt	I've lost my hat
paraplu	umbrella
kaas	cheese
het stinkt	it stinks
jas	coat
sjaal	scarf
broek	trousers
zonnebril	sunglasses
trui	sweater
schoenen	shoes
een	one
twee	two
drie	three
vier	four
vijf	five
computer	computer
boeken	books
sleutels	keys
bananen	bananas
fietsen	bicycles
Ik vind thee erg lekker	I love tea
bedankt	thank you
pruik	wig
rood	red
blond	blond
bruin	brown

groen	green
veelkleurig	multicoloured
hoed	hat
te hoog	too tall
te groot	too big
te klein	too small
te strak	too tight
ik heb mijn hoed gevonden	I've found my hat
heel erg bedankt	thank you very much
tot ziens	goodbye

THE WORLD OF
THE FABULOUS LOST & FOUND

THIS STORY IS ALSO AVAILABLE IN...

FRENCH

SPANISH

ITALIAN

CZECH

WELSH

KOREAN

GERMAN

HEBREW

SWEDISH

POLISH

SLOVAKIAN

VIETNAMESE

LATIN

PORTUGUESE

...AND MANY MORE LANGUAGES!

ENJOYED IT?
WRITE A REVIEW AND
LET US KNOW!

@MARK_PALLIS ON TWITTER
WWW.MARKPALLIS.COM

@PETERBAYNTON ON INSTAGRAM
WWW.PETERBAYNTON.COM

Made in the USA
Columbia, SC
26 March 2021